give THANKS

A JOURNAL FOR
SHARING GRATITUDE

JOSIE ROBINSON

ISBN: 978-1-945769-27-6

Printed in the United States of America
First Printing: 2016
20   19 18   17   16   5   4   3   2   1

Cover Design by Jessie Sayward Bright
Book Design by Kim Morehead

Wise Ink Creative Publishing
837 Glenwood Ave.
Minneapolis, MN 55405
www.wiseinkpub.com

"The greatest thing is to give thanks for everything. The person who has learned this knows what it means to live. They have penetrated the whole mystery of life: giving thanks for everything.

"We offer up thanksgiving this day for the fruits of the Earth. We thank God for the sunshine, but also for the hard rain that satisfies the thirst of Earth, for the driving wind that carries the pollen from one plant to another, for the cold that preserved the seed in the Earth, for the storms of spring that washed the land of snow and ice.

"Thus you give thanks to God not only for the happy and sunny events which ripen your life's fruit. Much that is sad and hard is also mixed in with life's blessings. And for that you must thank God, because it, too, has contributed to your spiritual growth.

"If life is such a burden that you feel crushed beneath it, then search out how you can thank God nonetheless. For sometimes we are blind to God's plan for us and receive our sight only when we try to thank Him."

—FROM NOBEL PEACE PRIZE-WINNER ALBERT SCHWEITZER'S SERMON FROM NOVEMBER 20, 1904, CALLED "GRATITUDE: THE SECRET TO LIFE."

CONTENTS

Gratitude *(noun)*: The state of being grateful; thankfulness. The quality of being thankful; readiness to show appreciation for and to return kindness.

❬❬❬❬❬❬

Synonyms: Gratefulness - appreciation - thankfulness - thanks

THE SECRET TO LIFE

"Gratitude is the sign of noble souls."

—AESOP

Several years ago, I hit bottom. Thirty pounds overweight, a closet drunk, barely able to scrape up enough money to pay the bills each month . . . I was a mess. Getting out of bed each day to take care of my two small children was a huge chore. It got so dark, I was convinced my family would be better off without me, and I wanted out of my life. Permanently. I didn't know how to change these negative feelings but desperately wanted to. So, in a moment of pure heartache, I prayed. One of those pleading, crying, please-get-me-out-of-this-mess prayers.

God answered.

The answer to my prayer came through an incredible journey involving a wise spiritual guru named Maleah, an old jar, and my adorable little four-year-old son, Lucas. I documented my story from rock bottom to enlightenment in a book called *The Gratitude Jar: A Simple Guide to Creating*

Miracles. Through this amazing adventure I found the pathway to happiness, inner peace, and emotional freedom.

The secret to life, I discovered, was through the daily practice of gratitude.

My then four-year-old son, Lucas, and I did a 30-day gratitude practice together that completely changed our lives. As a result of using this gratitude practice, I reversed everything I had been struggling with: I lost my extra weight, finally got sober after countless failed attempts in the past, went from having a net worth of zero to tripling my income, strengthened my relationships with every single person around me, rekindled my faith, and became a joyous, content, and peaceful person for perhaps the first time ever.

All because of a simple gratitude practice.

In this journal, you'll learn step-by-step how to use the exact same gratitude practice I used along with several other simple yet powerful practices that will deepen your transformation even further.

In a nutshell, this gratitude journal will change your life.

CHANGE YOUR THOUGHTS, CHANGE YOUR LIFE

You now hold in your hands the key to living the life you've always dreamed of . . .

- To feel happier, lighter.

- To be more connected in your personal relationships.
- To attract greater abundance and prosperity.
- To dramatically decrease your stress levels.
- To restore your mental, emotional, physical, and spiritual health.
- To greatly expand your creativity.
- To live your highest and best purpose, every single day.

All this and more is possible by spending a few minutes each day in gratitude.

I know, I know . . . it all sounds too good to be true, right? You might think I'm exaggerating, but I'm definitely not. I get messages from readers all over the world about how reading *The Gratitude Jar* changed their lives, or the life of someone they'd given a copy to, and how x, y, z incredible thing had happened as a result of using the gratitude practice inside its pages. Gratitude *works*.

Someone once told me gratitude is the most powerful prayer we can offer, to which I say, absolutely. There's nothing more powerful than saying thank you, for everything. God loves that stuff. At least that was my experience—God showered me with crazy-amazing joy, abundance, and straight-up miracles once I started spending time each day in gratitude, thanking God for all that is. Gratitude truly is the secret to life, as Nobel Peace Prize–winner Albert Schweitzer so eloquently stated at the opening of this journal.

I still don't know how gratitude works so magically, but that's probably okay. God likes us to have a little mystery when it comes to these things, I suppose. What I do know is that practicing gratitude will create huge shifts within your life, and I truly believe that experiencing gratitude on a daily basis will bring about more positive changes than any other thing you've tried before. It certainly did for me and for the countless others who've reached out to me with their own amazing transformation stories.

And the good news is . . . things keep getting better . . . and better . . . and better . . . when you continue using this practice in your life. I've discovered that as I continue to live in gratitude, things continue to spiral to new and greater heights. My bliss is at an all-time high. It's truly amazing.

I'm very excited about this grand gratitude adventure you're about to embark on, and I'm honored to be your "gratitude guide." Bad pun, I know. But it's fitting. As someone who has fully immersed themselves in the healing power of gratitude—as well as spoken with countless people who've had major transformations in their lives as a result of using the practices inside this journal—I feel somewhat qualified for the job.

I promise that by the end of this adventure you'll be uplifted in some small, or very large, way. Things will be different for you somehow. For some of you things will be very different . . . but in the very best possible ways.

So are you ready to change your life?

Thought so.

Let the miracles begin.

With love & GRATITUDE,

—Josie Robinson
Author of *The Gratitude Jar: A Simple Guide to Creating Miracles*

HOW TO USE THIS JOURNAL:
90 DAYS OF GIVING THANKS

There are 90 days total in this journal for you to write your gratitudes, with two pages given for each day. (You'll learn why there are two pages instead in the instructions on the following pages. There's an important reason.) You can choose to do your gratitude practice for all 90 days continuously, or break it up into three 30-day cycles.

I'm a big believer in the magic of 30-day cycles. There's proof all around us (in the moon's phases for example) that there's a naturally occurring 30-day renewal cycle, that we can use to strengthen the cycles of transformation in our lives. My mentor, who originally taught me about the power of gratitude, suggested 30 days for the practice, and I've kept it as a guideline ever since—that's why I recommend breaking your practice up into three 30-day cycles, so you can take advantage of this natural process to greatly enhance your results.

For me personally, I do three 30-day cycles spaced-out throughout the year because that works best for me. Normally I do a 30-day cycle in the 30 days leading up to Easter or around spring solstice, another 30-day cycle in the summertime, and then another cycle in the 30 days leading up to Christmas. It seems as if when the seasons change, I feel geared up to renew my gratitude practice. But it may be different for you.

Obviously you can choose to practice gratitude the full 90 days if you wish to. Do whatever feels natural to you. That's why I leave it open because honestly, it doesn't really matter how you practice gratitude—all that matters is that you practice it at all.

Either way, 30 days seems to be the magic number to turn your gratitude practice into a permanent habit and to gain all the benefits available, which is why I recommend trying the practice for at least one cycle of 30 days, and seeing what happens (PS: miracles will).

So what do you do for your 90 days of gratitude?

All you have to do is Give THANKS.

THE LIFE-CHANGING, MIRACLE-MAKING, GIVE THANKS FORMULA

Give THANKS
Think about what you're grateful for.
Have an open mind.
Allow yourself to feel gratitude.
Note your gratitude.
Keep it in your journal, or other special place.
Share it with someone else.

Consider Give THANKS to be your roadmap for your gratitude adventure. I created Give THANKS so you can gain the most benefits possible from using a gratitude practice. Plus, it's super simple. This is the basic formula you'll use throughout this gratitude journal.

Each day, select a time to complete the Give THANKS formula. I personally practice Give THANKS at the end of the day as my wind-down ritual (plus, research shows that practicing gratitude at bedtime helps you sleep better), but I know many people who like to Give THANKS in the morning to start their day off in a positive direction. Either way is wonderful and life changing. Just pick whichever way works best for you and your life.

GIVE THANKS

Think about what you're grateful for. For this first step, all you need to do is simply reflect on what you're most grateful for. Think about what's happening in your life at the moment; reflect on the people you know, where you live and work, your day-to-day events. Is something standing out? That's your gratitude for the day.

Have an open mind. Don't judge whatever comes up. Be open to whatever your heart and your intuition tell you to be thankful for. Giving gratitude for anything, no matter how silly or small you think it may be, is powerful.

Allow yourself to feel gratitude. Once you've come up with your gratitude for the day, allow yourself to let the *feeling* of gratitude come into your body. Gratitude is a powerful healing emotion that will instantly release your stress and tension—let it linger in your heart for a little while. Take some deep breaths and enjoy the feeling.

Note your gratitude. Write down your gratitude, because there's power in the act of writing it down and making it physical. Write, "I'm thankful for _____ today because . . . " and fill in as many details as possible.

I should note that this journal is unlined because—and while I don't have any scientific research to prove what I'm about to say, I've found it to be true for myself and many others—I think writing without lines is preferable for gratitude practices. It subconsciously opens you up to be more creative and heart-centered. Lines are logical and left-brained, and that's not the space we're aiming for. Blank sheets of paper are liberating for your mind, heart, and soul.

Don't worry if your handwriting is messy, or it's not all centered on the page. It doesn't matter. In fact, if it is a bit haphazard, that's great—it's not supposed to be perfect, not even a bit. Just let go, and write your gratitudes however they come out. Feel free to put a little doodle on the page too if you wish. The point is, flow and have fun with it. Write from your heart.

Keep it in a special place. I like physical items like jars and journals to hold my gratitudes, because when you have them lying around your home, you get a boost of gratitude every time you see them. Plus, whenever you need a pick-me-up, you can read through some of your journal entries for an instant burst of joy and goodness. There's something about being able to hold gratitude in your hands that's really special, which is why I encourage you to store it in a physical place.

Share it with someone else. Sharing your gratitude practice with another person is amazingly powerful, and I sincerely believe it will greatly enhance your results. I've left two pages of space each day, so there's room for you and a partner to write out your different gratitudes. Here are some ideas for sharing your gratitude journal if you need inspiration:

- One mom I know kept her journal sitting on the kitchen counter; she and her teenage daughter would write in it before they left the house for the day. Then, during dinnertime, they would read their gratitudes together.
- Two good friends of mine who lived long-distance from each other would call each other every night for 30 days and write in their own gratitude journals.
- Post your gratitude online on your favorite social media site.
- I've seen Give THANKS shared in hospitals, schools, and rehabilitation centers as a powerful therapeutic activity.

Of course you can use this gratitude journal on your own if you'd like to, and if you do you'll still experience all the wonderful benefits that a daily gratitude practice provides. But in my opinion, sharing gratitude with another person is pure miracle-making. Something really special happens when two or more people get together and share gratitude, or any other sacred, spiritual thing.

Things start *moving*.

The point is, try to make this step work as best you can, because as the old Swedish proverb says: Happiness shared is happiness doubled. Pure magic lies in this step.

If it's just not possible to share this with someone else, that's completely okay. Maybe you just share one of your 30-day cycles with someone else, and your other two are on your own. I've used Give THANKS on my own several times, especially when I'm doing one of the modified versions of the practice, which I'll explain in the next section.

All that really matters is that you Give THANKS in the way that works best for you. Any way you decide to Give THANKS will cause good, amazing, wonderful things to happen in your life.

"Gratitude is one of the sweet shortcuts to finding peace of mind and happiness inside. No matter what is going on outside of us, there's always something we could be grateful for."

—BARRY NEIL KAUFMAN

VARIATIONS ON GIVE THANKS

In this journal, there are 90 days total for Giving THANKS, and I recommend for the first 30 days doing the basic Give THANKS formula to get familiar the format. Then, you can decide if you'd like to stick with the basic formula, or if you wish to move onto the more advanced gratitude practices found in this section.

If you decide to continue with the basic Give THANKS formula for the full 90 days of this journal, I've included some writing prompts each week that you can choose to use if you'd like. Sometimes it helps to have a little direction, even if you're keeping it open and using the basic formula.

After you've used the basic Give THANKS formula for at least one 30 day cycle, listen to your intuition for which Give THANKS practice to continue on with. Your intuition will steer you in the right direction of which Give THANKS practice will serve your highest and best purpose.

The best way to figure out which Give THANKS practice is the right one to continue on with is to notice how you feel while you read through each of these practices. Is there one that makes you excited, curious, goosebumpy?

That's the one you should do.

"One becomes a buddha the moment one accepts all that life brings, with gratitude."

—OSHO

VARIATION ONE

*"When you change the way you look at things,
the things you look at change."*

—ESTHER HICKS

GIVE THANKS IN ONE AREA

This is one of my favorite variations, and I've used it several times for many different areas of my life. Each time I've used it, I've had a complete transformation with the area I've focused on; I've heard the same thing from many others who have also used this practice themselves. Dream jobs come out of the blue, difficult relationships untangle, random checks come in the mail, chronic illnesses heal, and so on.

This practice makes magic happen, quickly.

INSTRUCTIONS

Pick an area of life you feel "stuck" in—money, relationships, career, health, or any other—and use the Give THANKS formula for 30 days in that specific area.

My sister-in-law, Emma, was the person who originally came up with this idea. She had used the basic Give THANKS formula many times and had experienced huge positive shifts across the board—but still felt stuck around money. It just wasn't flowing like she wanted it to. So, Emma decided to Give THANKS for 30 days and focused specifically on the area of money and abundance.

If someone bought her a cup of coffee, or she found a penny in the street, she gave gratitude about it. If the vegetables in her garden were growing, she gave gratitude about that too. When her dad came over with dinner one evening, another gratitude. Any time she felt abundance was coming her way in any form, that was her gratitude for the day. After a few weeks of Giving THANKS for abundance, the money miracles started happening.

She called me about halfway through her 30 days to share some of the blessings that were showing up in her life. Emma was practically breathless as she told me that when she went to her mailbox that morning, there had been a check from her mother for $5,000 waiting. When Emma called her mom to find out why she received such a large check, her mom said it was because Emma's grandmother had recently sold her condo and wanted to share the proceeds from the sale with the family. Emma was one of the recipients. She couldn't believe it.

But that was just the beginning.

Emma went on to tell me that her consulting business had doubled almost overnight. She was booking new clients left and right, and one of her regular clients actually insisted Emma raise her rates because she wanted to "pay Emma what she was worth," which, according to her client, was a lot more than Emma was asking for. So Emma raised her rates and found it increased her business exponentially. Money was now flowing to Emma easily and effortlessly.

But most importantly, Emma said that her stress around money had disappeared, and she felt a sense of peace that her needs would always be taken care of. She had unblocked her money block, so to speak.

In *The Gratitude Jar* I devoted a whole chapter to how I used this practice to go from being almost unemployed and struggling to pay bills each month to having my ideal job handed to me on a silver platter and tripling my income. It was all due to giving gratitude around the area of my career and money, two areas I had been "stuck" in for several years.

What I learned from that experience (and continue to learn every time I practice this) is that giving thanks for what you want produces more of it, while thinking and complaining about what you don't want produces more of that. Spiritual leaders and gurus have been saying it for centuries, but I never actually believed them until I started practicing gratitude on a consistent basis. Now this has been proven to me time and again, and I know they're 100% right about the fact that your thoughts really do create your reality.

This is my go-to practice when things just aren't flowing in a certain area, and it works like a charm every single time.

Try it yourself, and see what happens. I promise you'll be pleasantly surprised by what shows up in your life.

"You can tell right now how much you have actually used gratitude in your life. Just take a look at all the major areas in your life: money, health, happiness, career, home, and relationships. The areas of your life that are abundant and wonderful are where you have used gratitude and are experiencing the magic as a result. Any areas that are not abundant and wonderful are due to a lack of gratitude.

"Most certainly you have been grateful at various times in your life, but to see the magic and cause a radical change to your current circumstances, you have to practice gratitude and make it your new way of life."

—FROM *THE MAGIC* BY RHONDA BYRNE

VARIATION TWO

"Love doesn't make the world go round. Love is what makes the ride worthwhile."

—FRANKLIN P. JONES

GIVE THANKS: THE LOVE NOTES JAR & THE LOVE LIST

At my live talks, after I share with people about the power of giving gratitude in one area, I usually get several questions on how to use Give THANKS specifically for love relationships. I tell people that you can use the previous practice and focus on the area of love—be it love for your partner, children, friends, or yourself—and it will work wonders for your relationships across the board. But readers still wanted something more, so I created not one, but two different practices that you can use to expand the love in your life.

The first practice is for those of you already in a love relationship, and the second is for attracting a new love if you're single. Both practices will increase the love in your life exponentially.

THE LOVE NOTES JAR
(FOR COUPLES)

I have my friend Melanie to thank for this first beautiful practice. Melanie used this practice years ago at the very beginning stages of her relationship. When she finished, she gave it to her husband, Tom, as a one-year anniversary gift. Ten years into their relationship, Melanie told me that Tom still considers it one of the best gifts he's ever received, and every year on their anniversary they read through their love notes together.

Melanie used a jar for this practice, which you can use also, or you can write your love notes in this journal. As many of you know, I love using jars for my gratitude practices, so I had to include at least one jar in this journal somewhere. They're just so lovely.

INSTRUCTIONS

1. **Get a jar (or use your journal).** Melanie used a jar that you can write on, which can be purchased at a craft store or an online specialty shop. She wrote a short description of what was inside the jar on the outside of it. You could also just use a plain jar with a note describing what's inside the jar. If you're using your journal, you can simply write your love notes inside your journal on the pages provided.

2. **Cut up little slips of paper in three different colors.** Melanie used red, yellow, and green—but you can use whatever colors are your favorite or that you have on hand.

Designate a paper color to go with each statement:

Red paper: Things I love about you.
Green paper: Special memories we've shared.
Yellow paper: Hopes for our future together.

If you're using your journal instead of a jar, you could use three different colors of pens for your three areas if you wish.

3. **Write your notes, fold them in half, and put into the jar.** Melanie said many of her notes were really simple—just a sentence or two for each.

4. **Share with your partner.** There are many ways to share this practice with your partner: You both could do this practice together for 30 days and write your three love notes each day, sharing them aloud with each other as you complete them. Or you could do this practice yourself and give it to your partner as a gift like Melanie did. Either way is powerful.

Do share this practice with your partner in whatever way feels best for the both of you. This step, especially for this practice, is very important. It will open up a brand-new channel of conversation within your relationship.

I remember reading years ago that couples who told "positive" relationship stories about themselves stayed together longer and were significantly happier than couples who told negative stories. This is a simple way to tell your story in a positive light.

My guess is that once you do this practice with your partner, it will open them up to remembering their own special memories of you, memories you may have forgotten that will only add to your love story. And by focusing on your hopes for the future, you'll ensure that your love story continues for many years to come.

THE LOVE LIST
(FOR ATTRACTING NEW LOVE)

In all these Give THANKS variations, a common element is getting you to think about what you *want*, instead of what you *don't* want. Many of us are good at thinking about what we don't want in our lives, especially with a potential love partner, but that can backfire—the more we focus on what we don't want, the more we bring it into our lives. Likewise, by thinking about and giving gratitude for what we want, we bring that into our lives.

For this practice, you're going to focus on what you want in your future partner. This will help in attracting someone with these traits into your life. Trust me, it works. I used this practice myself many, many years ago and met my amazing husband, Shawn, shortly after I completed it.

INSTRUCTIONS

1. **Every day for 30 days, Give THANKS for the qualities you'd be grateful for your future partner to have.** Think about what it is you want in a future partner, and Give THANKS for that specific thing each day.

2. **Write your gratitudes in the present tense.** For example, write, "I'm grateful my partner is kind and treats me with compassion," or "I'm grateful my partner shares my zany sense of humor and we can make each other laugh." Think about the specific qualities that you value the most, that you look for in your closest friends, or that were absent from partners in past love relationships, and write them down in this format: "I'm grateful my partner is . . . " Fill it in as completely as possible.

When you write your gratitudes in the present, and when you get specific about what you're grateful for, you're using the law of attraction to turn yourself into a magnet for receiving exactly what you want, or even better.

3. **Share this list with a trusted friend or family member.** You could have another single friend do this practice together with you for 30 days, or you could read all your gratitudes out loud to someone at the end of your practice. Do whatever feels most comfortable for you. But try to complete this step, because it's very powerful. As I've said time and again, the magic lies in this part of the process. Writing things down and sharing them with someone else is when the miracles happen.

Personally, I think doing this practice with another single friend would be lots of fun. Calling each other each night, or getting together over coffee or cocktails and talking about your future dream person . . . fun! That's how it's supposed to feel when you're doing these practices. Like play. Because that fun, joyful play state is where we create the most positive change in our lives.

I myself wrote a Love List a full year before I met my husband, Shawn. I wrote down all the qualities I would be grateful for my future partner to have with a friend of mine, who was also single at the time. We both had a lot of giggles about our lists, then tucked them away in a drawer.

A year later, I had completely forgotten about my Love List until I met

Shawn. A few months after Shawn and I had started dating, I pulled out that list and realized he fit every single thing I had written (and I had written a lot).

*"Being deeply loved by someone gives you strength,
while loving someone deeply gives you courage."*

—LAO TZU

VARIATION THREE

"If you're alive, you're a creative person."

—ELIZABETH GILBERT

GIVE THANKS: ART JOURNAL

Some of you might see the word "art" in the title of this practice and immediately want to dismiss it because you don't consider yourself to be an artist or a creative-type person.

Please don't dismiss it. You don't have to be an artist, not even a tiny bit, to do this practice.

All you need to be is open-minded to the possibility that every single person is creative in their own way, and you can use your own creativity to express your gratitude. In this practice, I really want to encourage you to find some way to express your creativity—I believe that everyone has a creative spark within them, and finding this spark can be life-changing.

I've told you that I've seen huge transformations from people who've started daily gratitude practices, right? Well, I've also seen major transformations in people who've started regular creative practices. You can imagine what happens when you combine these two powerful practices together . . . simply amazing, breathtaking, wonderful things. Truly.

Being creative and grateful is when you move beyond the ordinary, into the extraordinary.

Like I always say, just give it a try and see what happens. I promise—with this Give THANKS variation, you will cause some major rumblings in your life, in a very good way.

INSTRUCTIONS

1. **Express your gratitudes through a creative outlet of your choosing, for 30 days or for 30 projects.** Each day, or each project, do something creative for your gratitude. You could draw a picture of your gratitude or take a photo. Write a poem. Make up a dance. Whatever creative medium you feel drawn to. Or maybe try something you used to do creatively but have since abandoned.

   Please feel free to mix up the mediums within the practice; you could draw one day, do a poem the next, and dance it out the day after that. Whatever suits your fancy. The most important thing is to have fun with this practice and not judge whatever comes out of you. There's no pressure here to be perfect; in fact, that's not the point at all.

   The point of this practice is to get you into the act of creating, which is one of our most powerful expressions as human beings.

The list is endless on what you could create for your 30 gratitudes, but here are some ideas to get you started:

- Poetry
- Calligraphy
- Photography
- Painting
- Drawing
- Music
- Crafting
- Dance
- Sculpture
- Collage
- Textiles

If you're still feeling intimidated by these options, you could just dress up your gratitudes with fancy paper and special markers each day. That's what my friend Jess did. Jess wrote her gratitudes on nice card-stock paper, then made a pretty frame out of different-colored paper for each one. She then took photos of them and shared them online. They turned out beautifully.

They were so beautiful that Jess turned her 30 gratitude papers into a keepsake book that she now keeps on her coffee table and reads through for inspiration on a regular basis. The coolest part is that even though Jess said that she "didn't have an artistic bone in her entire body" when she started her practice, she's now trying out new creative projects because the experience was so powerful and awakened something within her.

See? Magic.

Now, for those of you who are working artists or who have been involved in creating things for some time, this practice is an amazing opportunity to expand even further. One artist friend I know did an incredible project where she painted portraits of 30 artists who inspired her own artistic journey. Her paintings were her gratitude to each of them. She had her portraits featured on several media outlets and even went on to publish a book about them.

I'll admit, I'm a bit biased about this practice. My father was a high school art teacher and a brilliant artist himself, so I was raised around art, and it had a hugely positive impact on me. I know that being surrounded by so much creativity is a big reason why I decided to become a creative person myself. Personally, I think everyone could use a little more art in their lives. It really does make the world a more beautiful place to live in.

2. ***Optional* Share your journal with the world.** I left this optional because I know that just getting people, especially adults, to be creative in any way can be a challenge in itself. If the thought of sharing your creative gratitude projects makes you not want to do this practice, then don't share them. That's why this is optional, because I think the most important thing here is to be creative.

But to stay within the spirit of sharing gratitude, I'd like to encourage you to share your project with someone if you feel comfortable doing so. You could be bold and post it publically online, or you could keep it in a sketchbook or folder and show it to a trusted loved one.

Now, I realize I'm asking you to go off-roading outside this journal right now, but when it comes to art, sometimes you've got to go outside the lines. You definitely could use the space inside the journal to draw or paint, which is another reason why this journal is unlined, but this is one practice where I encourage you to step outside.

Get some fancy paper. Or huge sheets of white paper. Neon paper. Colorful paints or markers. Crayons. Glitter. Beautiful fabric.

And have fun.

*"The essence of all beautiful art,
all great art, is gratitude. "*

—FRIEDRICH NIETZSCHE

VARIATION FOUR

"Never forget the three powerful resources you always have available to you: love, prayer, and forgiveness."

—H. JACKSON BROWN, JR.

GIVE THANKS: FORGIVENESS

practiced this recently and can honestly say it was one of the most powerful things I've done—and I've had some pretty big transformational experiences in my life. We always hear how important it is to forgive others, as well as ourselves, but we get stuck on how exactly to do that. I know I felt stuck, anyway. But this practice helped me forgive someone who I'd been unable to for many, many years.

There was a person in my life (whom I shall keep confidential), whom I was holding a lot of hurt toward that I couldn't seem to let go. I wanted to let it go, but I just couldn't. So I prayed on it, and the answer came that I should do a gratitude practice around this person. This seems to be my solution from above for almost everything, but that's probably because these gratitude practices work such big miracles for me.

Anyway, I did a 30-day gratitude practice around the person I was holding all the negativity toward, and it totally shifted something inside me. By the end of it, I felt freer, lighter. And I was finally—after about a decade of holding onto anger, resentment, sadness, and guilt around this person and our relationship—able to let it go completely.

I also discovered that this practice dramatically changed our relationship dynamic together—so much so that the last time I saw this person I felt an overwhelming love and kindness toward them, which was a huge change from how I usually felt. I gave them a hug and told them how grateful I was that they were part of my life. Before, things had always been tense and uncomfortable between us. Now, amazingly, they weren't. It was a really powerful moment for the both of us, and I know it never would have happened had I not done this practice.

I highly, highly recommend this practice if you're having a difficult time with forgiveness, either with someone in your life or with yourself. I promise that by the end of the practice you'll see things from a different perspective.

INSTRUCTIONS

1. **Each day for 30 days, write down something you're grateful for about the person you're trying to forgive.** When I was doing this practice myself, I would take a deep breath, clear my mind of any negativity, and then visualize the person I wanted to forgive. I know how hard it can be to call up gratitude around someone who's caused you pain—that's why I recommend getting into a calm state of mind before you begin.

Try to come up with something, anything, you're grateful for around this person. For many of us this is someone we were in a love relationship with, a close family member, or a friend we've known many years. Because it's someone you've likely had a deep relationship with, chances are there are some good memories mixed in with the not-so-good ones that may have defined your relationship near the end. Try to call to mind memories from happier times or when the person was at their best. Continue to take deep breaths and remain in a calm, peaceful space while you think of your gratitude.

I should note that I included being grateful for some of the "negative" things this person did throughout the course of our relationship, because, as I got deeper into this practice, I realized that these difficult things actually caused me to develop many positive qualities, qualities I never would have developed had it not been for this relationship and the challenges that came with it. This was a surprising revelation for me and made me see things in a totally new light.

If you're having a difficult time coming up with a gratitude, you can pray for God to reveal it to you. Trust me, God will.

2. **Do a special "bless and release" ceremony when you've finished the practice.** When I was done with my 30 days of gratitude and forgiveness, I felt I needed to do something to give it closure. So I called my sister over for a bonfire at my backyard fire pit, and we had a little ceremony together. I read aloud each of my 30 gratitudes to her, and after I read each one, I threw it into the fire. She also read her own 30 gratitudes out loud to me and threw them in the fire because she had done her own forgiveness practice, only hers was about forgiving her-

self. There were lots of tears, laughter, and meaningful conversation.

When we were done sharing our gratitudes and tossing them all into the fire, I said a final prayer that went something like this:

"I completely forgive you, (person's name), and completely release all negative attachments to you. Thank you for the role you've played in my life, but I'm ready to release you completely in love, gratitude, and forgiveness. I give it all to God right now to bless and release. Thank you. Amen."

And that was it. Once we finished our ceremony, my sister and I talked about how we both felt like we'd just lost about twenty-five pounds each. All the emotional baggage we'd both been carrying for so many years just went poof in the fire.

Now, you don't have to do a fire ceremony like my sister and I did; just saying a simple prayer or affirmation at the end of your 30 days of forgiveness will do. Feel free to do whatever feels intuitive to you. Light a candle and say a little prayer. Go somewhere beautiful in nature and spend time in reflection. Call a trusted friend or family member over, read your gratitudes to them, and pray together for closure.

It doesn't really matter what you choose as your ceremony, but it is important to say or do something out loud to acknowledge that you forgive and release completely. It gives special power to it.

"When you hold resentment toward another, you are bound to that person or condition by an emotional link that is stronger than steel. Forgiveness is the only way to dissolve that link and get free."

—CATHERINE PONDER

VARIATION FIVE

*"Whenever there's a grateful moment, I note it.
I know for sure that appreciating whatever shows up
for you in life changes your whole world. You radiate
and generate more goodness for yourself when you're
aware of all you have and not focusing on your
have-nots.*

*"I know for sure: if you make time for a little
gratitude every day, you'll be amazed by the results."*

—FROM *WHAT I KNOW FOR SURE*
BY OPRAH WINFREY

GIVE THANKS: 5 THINGS

I consider this variation to be the "classic" way to practice gratitude. In all the research studies on the benefits of gratitude, this is usually the practice researchers have participants use (PS: researchers have found in study after study that the benefits from this practice, and any other gratitude practice, are incredible). I also included this variation in *The Gratitude Jar* because it's so simple, yet so powerful.

This is the gratitude practice that Oprah Winfrey herself uses, so you know it's a good one.

INSTRUCTIONS

Write down five things you're thankful for at the end of each day. Every night before bedtime, reflect back on your day and think about five things that happened that you're grateful for. These five things can be anything—from the completely mundane to the really special.

Feel free to write as much as you want; some people I know just write one word for each of their gratitudes, and others write full journal entries. Do what works best for you, but try to come up with five. That seems to be the magic number.

This is a practice that I always come back to whenever I need a quick boost of gratitude or if I'm having a tough time getting to sleep. It calms me right down and gets me in a good frame of mind to drift off to dreamland.

"In a series of studies, my colleagues and I have helped people systematically cultivate gratitude, usually by keeping a 'gratitude journal' in which they regularly record the things for which they're grateful.

"Gratitude journals and other gratitude practices often seem so simple and basic; in our studies, we often have people keep gratitude journals for just three weeks. And yet the results have been overwhelming. We've studied more than one thousand people, from ages eight to 80, and found that people who practice gratitude consistently report a host of benefits:

Physical

Stronger immune systems
Less bothered by aches and pains
Lower blood pressure
Exercise more and take better care of their health
Sleep longer and feel more refreshed upon waking

Psychological

Higher levels of positive emotions
More alert, alive, and awake
More joy and pleasure
More optimism and happiness

Social

More helpful, generous, and compassionate
More forgiving
More outgoing
Feel less lonely and isolated

"The social benefits are especially significant here because, after all, gratitude is a social emotion. I see it as a relationship-strengthening emotion because it requires us to see how we've been supported and affirmed by other people.

"Indeed, this cuts to the very heart of my definition of gratitude, which has two components. First, it's an affirmation of goodness. We affirm that there are good thing in the world, gifts and benefits we've received. This doesn't mean that life is perfect; it doesn't ignore complaints, burdens, and hassles. But when we look at life as a whole, gratitude encourages us to identify some amount of goodness in our lives.

"The second part of gratitude is figuring out where that goodness comes from. We recognize the sources of this goodness as being outside of ourselves. It didn't stem from anything we necessarily did ourselves in which we might take pride. We can appreciate positive traits in ourselves, but I think true gratitude involves a humble dependence on others: We acknowledge that other people—or even higher powers, if you're of a spiritual mindset—gave

us many gifts, big and small, to help us achieve the goodness in our lives."

—FROM THE ARTICLE, "WHY GRATITUDE IS GOOD" WRITTEN BY DR. ROBERT EMMONS, THE WORLD'S LEADING SCIENTIFIC EXPERT ON GRATITUDE

VARIATION SIX

*"Let us be grateful to the people
who make us happy; they are the charming
gardeners who make our souls blossom."*

—MARCEL PROUST

GIVE THANKS: THANK-YOU NOTES

This practice was inspired by a lawyer named John Kralik, who wrote a book called *A Simple Act of Gratitude: How Learning to Say Thank You Changed My Life*. John wrote a thank-you note every day over the course of a year and documented his experience in a book. As you can probably imagine, doing this thank-you note practice completely changed John's life. This is another favorite of mine from *The Gratitude Jar*. I love this practice because it can impact so many people in a positive, beautiful way.

INSTRUCTIONS

Write a thank-you note to someone every day for the next 30 days. Think of people who have made a positive impact on you or just did something nice for you one day. Try to think of as many people as you can: friends, family, coworkers, service workers, anyone that you encounter during any given day that has touched you in some way.

Tell them how their actions or gifts have affected you, even if it was something simple like holding open the door for you or giving you a friendly smile. You can be as long or short with your thank-you notes as you wish. Mention the next time you might see them, or just let them know you're thinking of them. End with your warm regards. I recommend writing your note in your journal first, then get some pretty thank-you cards to copy it onto. Send your thank you note in the mail, or give it to the person by hand.

One of my good friends sent me a random thank-you note in the mail a few years ago, telling me how grateful she was that I was her friend and some other kind things. I was so moved by the gesture and still have the card, years later. I got to experience a huge burst of gratitude when I received her thank-you note, so it's a blessing for both the giver and the receiver.

"The best thank-you notes will stir in the recipients' hearts the knowledge that their gesture was truly appreciated, and even inspire the desire to give again, knowing that they will be thanked and appreciated.

"The one sure piece of advice I have on how to write thank-you notes is this: write a lot of them. Many of the notes I wrote at the beginning of the year provoked the biggest reaction because people were, frankly, in shock that I had written them. Some of the notes later in the year were more apt, got directly to the heart of what I wanted to say to my correspondents, and showed that I could sincerely appreciate and understand them and their efforts. There was, occasionally, a certain eloquence to them.

"At the risk of making an unscientific and directly moral statement, I will say that writing thank-you notes is a good thing to do and makes the world a better place. It also made me a better man. More than success or material achievement, this is what I sought."

—FROM *A SIMPLE ACT OF GRATITUDE: HOW LEARNING TO SAY THANK YOU CHANGED MY LIFE* BY JOHN KRALIK

VARIATION SEVEN

*"A single thankful thought toward heaven
is the most perfect of all prayers."*

—GOTTHOLD EPHRAIM LESSING

GIVE THANKS: THE GOD BOX

Every major spiritual text is filled with verses about expressing gratitude to God, and I believe that is because it's the best way to reach Him. Something I talk about in *The Gratitude Jar* is the way it seemed as if every time I gave gratitude, even for the littlest thing, I felt that I touched a presence greater than myself. It's like gratitude opened the channel between me and God, and I could touch God if only for a minute. Gratitude opened my eyes to finally see all the blessings God had been giving me my whole life—I just never noticed them before.

When I could see my world through the eyes of gratitude, I discovered that God answered my prayers in some way or another every single time I prayed. Maybe it wasn't exactly how I expected it, but God always, always, always answered.

I also found when I acknowledged God with gratitude for answering my prayers, my blessings multiplied. So did my joy.

For this practice, it's all about thanking and acknowledging the amazing Creator who made it all possible. In my humble opinion, it's the least we can do. This practice will help you to notice how much God is present in your life and see how God answers your prayers, all the time.

INSTRUCTIONS

1. **Write down your prayer, then give it to God.** You can write your prayer in your journal or on a blank sheet of paper and put it in a "God Box," which is exactly what it sounds like. It could be an actual box, a basket, or even a jar (of course I had to sneak another jar in here somewhere). The point is, keep your prayer somewhere physical so you can refer back to it when God answers.

    This first step is as simple as it sounds—if you have a prayer, be it for a relationship, health, career, spirituality, or anything else, write it down. You can write your prayer however you wish; this is an exercise I don't have a writing prompt for because I think prayers are best left open. Just write what you feel, and don't worry if you're saying the exact right thing. God will understand.

    Once you're done writing your prayer, give it to God by saying it out loud and acknowledging that you're now giving it to God. Ask God to answer in a way that serves the highest purpose of everyone involved, or simply say, "I give this prayer to you, God."

I've found when I leave my prayers open-ended and let God figure it out, instead of trying to force things a certain way, it always turns out much better. If I say to God, "I'd like you to answer my prayer by this really specific thing happening . . . ," it's not as good as when I just let God do God's thing. In my experience, God will come up with such an elegant solution, something I never would've thought of on my own, that now I always just let go and let God when I pray.

Once you've said your prayer and given it to God, relax and know that God will answer in Divine Time.

2. **Write down your gratitude every time your prayer is answered.** Be on the lookout after you've let your prayer go—I've noticed God usually answers my prayers through people, signs, books, and dreams. Often my solution is presented through a conversation with someone I "happen" to run into; books pop off the shelf with the exact information I need; or I'll have a vivid, prophetic dream. Sometimes, I'll be out for a walk and an eagle will fly overhead—that's my sign that the Spirit is guiding me. God answers in all kinds of ways; some are direct, and some are more symbolic. Either way, when you feel like God is answering your prayer in any way, write it down.

You can simply write, "Thank you God for answering my prayer through this person, event, sign, etc.," then write a little about the way your prayer was answered. You can put your gratitude in your God Box, or keep it in your journal. What I usually do for this practice is use two pages of my journal; one page is for my prayers and the other page is for the answers I receive.

By practicing this, you'll start to see that God communicates with us in all kinds of ways—we usually miss it because we're not paying close enough attention. You'll also begin to see the way God communicates with you personally. Maybe it's through music, or meditation, or hunches and nudges from your intuition. I think it's unique for everyone, but by doing this practice you'll open up to your Higher guidance and wisdom and realize you're never truly alone in this universe.

3. ***Optional* Have a prayer partner.** You'll notice I mention my sister several times throughout this journal, and that's because she's been my prayer partner throughout the past few years. Having her as my prayer partner has been one of the most enriching parts of my life. A few years ago, she and I started going on walks during which we'd talk about how God was showing up in our lives. Both of us were going through huge changes at the time and felt we needed to find the higher insight into everything that was happening.

   We noticed as we walked and talked and prayed each week that the miracles in both our lives got bigger and bigger, to the point where every time we got together we'd say, "You won't even believe what happened this week!" Seriously amazing things. Sharing our prayers with each other, then talking about how they were being answered, made us feel so connected to each other and to God. It really opened our eyes to all the blessings and synchronicity that surrounded us. We've been doing this routine for several years, and I now consider my weekly "prayer walks" with my sister an important foundation of my spiritual life.

   Now, I left this part optional because I know it might be a challenge to find someone to be your prayer partner with how busy our lives are these days. However, if you can make this step work, I highly recommend it. Like I keep saying, sharing your gratitude, prayers, or any other sacred, spiritual thing with someone else is pure miracle-making.

It could be a simple chat on the phone each week, a morning ritual with your partner or children, meeting for coffee after a church service, or a weekly walk like my sister and I do. Just a simple conversation each week or each day about what your prayers are and how they're being answered is all it needs to be.

If you'd like a prayer partner but don't think you have anyone in your life to be that person, put it in your God Box, and let God find you someone. God will.

This is an ongoing practice for me, so I don't have a suggestion for doing it 30 days in a row or for a specific time frame. You can do this one whenever, wherever you need to. God is always available. Thank goodness.

"Gratitude gives us eyes to see God, Earth, beauty, love, joy, and abundance. Everything we never knew was already right there in front of us, waiting. We just needed gratitude to open our eyes."

—FROM *THE GRATITUDE JAR:*
A SIMPLE GUIDE TO CREATING MIRACLES

GIVE THANKS

"You simply will not be the same person two months from now after consciously giving thanks each day for the abundance that exists in your life. And you will have set in motion an ancient spiritual law: The more you have and are grateful for, the more will be given to you."

—SARAH BAN BREATHNACH

DAY

3

DAY

4

DAY

5

DAY

6

HOME

Choose three things around your home you're grateful to own. How do they make your life better? Maybe it's a comfy reading chair, a special piece of art, the view outside your window, or your nice, warm bed. What three things do you love the most about your space?

"He is happiest, be he king or peasant,
who finds peace in his home."

—JOHANN WOLFGANG VON GOETHE

DAY

7

DAY

8

DAY

9

DAY
10

DAY
11

DAY

12

FOOD

Write about something delicious that puts you into a state of instant, overwhelming gratitude the minute it enters your mouth. Maybe it's a special dish from a certain café or something you indulge in everyday. Whatever it is, write it down and go into detail about what it is and why you love it.

"Thank you for the food we eat,

Thank you for the world so sweet,

Thank you for the birds that sing,

Thank you God for everything."

—MEALTIME PRAYER

DAY
14

DAY

16

DAY
17

EARTH

I didn't notice how beautiful this planet was until I started practicing gratitude. Now, it's all I notice. Earth is incredible, and we are beyond lucky to call it our home. What about this amazing Earth are you most grateful for? Pick a beautiful place in nature to write your gratitude today.

"The best remedy for those who are afraid, lonely or unhappy, is to go outside, somewhere where they can be quiet, alone with the heavens, nature and God. Because only then does one feel that all is as it should be and that God wishes to see people happy, amidst the simple beauty of nature."

—ANNE FRANK

DAY

19

DAY

20

DAY
21

DAY
22

DAY

23

DAY
24

BODY

On those extra-tough days when it's difficult to find gratitude, there's always one thing you can call on: being alive. No matter what, if you're still here and participating in this journal, you have that. Thank your body today. What's working well in your body? What's your favorite part? It's so easy to take our bodies for granted, but it's our reason for living. Give it the gratitude it deserves.

"Keeping your body healthy is an expression of gratitude to the whole cosmos—the trees, the clouds, everything."

—THICH NHAT HANH

DAY
26

DAY
27

DAY
29

DAY
30

REST

Having things we do that help us unwind and slow down are incredibly important to finding balance in the hustle and bustle of life. Write down something you're grateful for that helps you slow down and find your inner calm.

"To have faith is to trust yourself to the water. When you swim you don't grab hold of the water, because if you do you will sink and drown. Instead you relax, and float."

—ALAN W. WATTS

DAY
31

DAY
32

DAY

33

DAY
34

DAY
36

FRIENDS

For today, write your gratitude about a friend (or two or three). Think about the qualities they have that you're most grateful for—their kindness, compassion, humor, and what it is you love about them the most. Maybe a specific story stands out—something they did that shows what a great friend they are. Write it down, and share it with them in a letter or by telling them in conversation.

"*Piglet sidled up to Pooh from behind.*

'Pooh!' he whispered.

'Yes, Piglet?'

'Nothing,' said Piglet, taking Pooh's paw.
'I just wanted to be sure of you.'"

—FROM *THE HOUSE AT POOH CORNER*
BY A.A. MILNE

DAY
37

DAY
38

DAY

39

DAY

41

DAY
42

OPPONENTS

Difficult people are often our greatest teachers in disguise. Think of someone in your life who is hard to get along with—and write down at least one quality they have that you're grateful for. Try to see this person from a higher perspective and to see what spiritual lesson they're teaching you.

"To learn from our enemies is the best pathway to loving them; for it makes us grateful to them."

—FRIEDRICH NIETZSCHE

DAY
43

DAY
46

DAY
47

DAY

48

CAREER

For years, my job and money were my biggest sources of stress—until I started practicing gratitude around those two areas specifically. Once I did that, everything changed. I landed my dream job and got a pay raise along with it. Money started to flow to me instead of away from me. It was incredible.

All because I started a gratitude practice around these two areas, instead of complaining about them, which is what I had been doing before that. Today, write down a list of what you're most grateful for about your career. This changed everything for me, and now my career is a constant source of joy.

"When you are grateful for the things that you want to come into your life (the perfect relationship, the dream job, absolute health, total abundance) before they actually appear, you are sending out a frequency to the Universe that you already have those things. The law of attraction does not know if you are imagining something or if it is real, so by giving heartfelt thanks for now, you must attract those things to you. This is an immutable law, and when used correctly it is unfailing in its response."

—FROM *THE SECRET GRATITUDE BOOK*
BY RHONDA BYRNE

DAY
49

DAY
50

DAY

51

DAY

52

DAY

53

DAY

54

ROUTINE

Most of us have routines we do every single day no matter what we've got planned. In those day-to-day moments, there are things we rely on to get us through each day that we typically don't even notice. Deodorant. Running water. Coffee. Things we just can't live without that we use. Every. Single. Day. What's something you're grateful for that you use every day and can't live without?

"Gratitude bestows reverence, allowing us to encounter everyday epiphanies, those transcendent moments of awe that change forever how we experience life and the world."

—JOHN MILTON

DAY
55

DAY

57

DAY
58

DAY

59

STRUGGLE

When we give gratitude for the challenges we've faced or are currently facing in our lives, we're able to discover the golden nugget of wisdom hiding inside of the struggle. And though it might not seem like it, especially in the midst of things, there is always a golden nugget somewhere inside the storm.

Think about any struggles you've experienced or are currently experiencing that you're grateful for . . . what have you learned and how have you grown? What's the golden nugget from that experience?

"No one is as capable of gratitude as one who has emerged from the kingdom of night."

—ELIE WIESEL

DAY

61

DAY

62

DAY

63

DAY

64

DAY

65

DAY
66

MOM

Of all the people you owe a debt of gratitude the most, it's your mom. Without our moms, we wouldn't be. So today, celebrate and appreciate the woman whom you call Mom.

I know for some of you, your mom isn't your biological mom, but a dear aunt, grandmother, family friend, or adopted mother. Include her in your gratitude, along with the mother who carried you in her womb—even if she wasn't present in your life. This might be tough, but it will be very healing. Today, send your mom a thank you letter or your thoughts of gratitude.

"God could not be everywhere,
so he created mothers."

—JEWISH PROVERB

DAY

67

DAY
68

DAY
69

DAY
70

DAD

You knew Dad was going to be next, right? Of course. Dads deserve our gratitude and love as well. The same rules apply as for Mom: either write a thank you letter to the person who's been the father in your life, or send your thoughts of gratitude.

*"My father didn't tell me how to live;
he lived, and let me watch him do it."*

—CLARENCE BUDINGTON KELLAND

DAY
73

DAY
73

DAY
74

DAY
75

DAY

76

GOD

We've given thanks to our earthly mom and dad; now it's time to give thanks to our heavenly one. For today's gratitude, tell God what you're most grateful for that God has provided. Write it in your journal, then share it aloud in prayer. Sometimes I like to just kneel in prayer and tell God a laundry list of things I'm grateful for, and I always feel a big burst of love right back.

Even for those of you who might not believe in a Higher Power, say your gratitude to the ethers. Say it to the air. Because we all exist somehow, and if it's not because of God, it's because of something. Either way, we owe that Something a debt of gratitude.

"Perhaps nothing helps us make the movement from our little selves to a larger world than remembering God in gratitude. Such a perspective puts God in view in all of life, not just in the moments we set aside for worship or spiritual disciplines. Not just in the moments when life seems easy."

—HENRI NOUWEN

DAY
77

DAY
79

DAY

80

TIME

Perspective is a powerful thing. Sometimes we don't notice how far we've come until we can look back and reflect upon it. For this gratitude, reflect on what's different in your life today than it was a year ago . . . what are you most grateful for that's changed?

"The moment one is capable of feeling grateful for both pain and pleasure, without any distinction, without any choice, simply feeling grateful for whatsoever is given . . . Because if it is given by God, it must have a reason in it. We may like it, we may not like it, but it must be needed for our growth. Winter and summer are both needed for growth. Once this idea settles in the heart, then each moment of life is gratitude.

"Let this become your meditation and prayer; thank God every moment—for laughter, for tears, for everything. Then you will see a silence arising in your heart that you have not known before. That is bliss."

—OSHO

DAY
83

DAY
84

WORDS

I love reading beautifully written words; they always lift my spirits. What inspirational words of wisdom are you most grateful for receiving? Maybe it's something powerful someone told you that you've never forgotten, or maybe it's a famous quote posted in your office. Write what words you're most grateful for and why.

*"A drop of ink may make
a million think."*

—GEORGE GORDON BYRON

DAY
85

DAY

87

DAY
88

DAY

89

"Every good deed done to others is a great force that starts an unending pulsation through time and eternity. We may not know it, we may never hear a word of gratitude or of recognition, but it will all come back to us in some form as naturally, as perfectly, as inevitably, as echo answers to sound.

"Perhaps not as we expect it, how we expect it, nor where, but sometime, somehow, somewhere, it comes back, as the dove that Noah sent from the Ark returned with its green leaf of revelation. Let us conceive of gratitude in its largest, most beautiful sense, that if we receive any kindness we are debtor, not merely to one person, but to the whole world."

—WILLIAM GEORGE JORDAN

THE END:
YOUR GRATITUDE STORY

"Reading books changes lives. So does writing them."

—SARAH BAN BREATHNACH

There's tons of research that shows writing about anything—be it gratitudes, goals, feelings, dreams, or anything in between—makes people happier, less stressed, and more productive and creative. Basically, writing is really good for you.

I discovered this myself when I wrote *The Gratitude Jar*. The process of writing about where I was before I began my gratitude practice (the gutter), during the transformation itself (much better), then afterwards (pure amazement), was a yearlong spiritual practice in itself. Writing my story was totally therapeutic and made me realize how much I'd transformed as a result of using this practice. Like gratitude, writing helped me see my life in a different way.

So to end this journal, I'm going to ask you to write about your transformation. Doing so will open your eyes to how much your life has changed since you began this gratitude journey.

I've left some blank pages here at the end for you to write your own gratitude story. This is meant to be a fun, creative exercise and not a school assignment or anything like that. When it comes to writing your story, just write the first thing that comes to mind, and don't think too hard on if you're doing it right or misspelling things. It doesn't matter. The act of putting your thoughts and feelings to paper is the most important thing and will give you all the benefits writing provides.

Begin your story by writing about where you were before you started your gratitude practice—was there something that drew you to this journal in the first place? Did something need to change in your life, or did you feel like you needed to change somehow? Think back to where things were when you began, and write down how you were feeling and what was happening in your life at the time. Write as much as you can, and reflect honestly on where you were at.

Next, flash forward to today and take a look at where you're at right now. How have things changed? How have you changed? Do you notice anything big or little that's shifted in your life since you started using your gratitude practice? Maybe it's just feeling a bit happier and less stressed about things; or it could be something larger, like a job change or new relationship. Feel free to make a list if there have been a lot of changes. Take a look at all the areas of your life—career, relationships, health, abundance, spirituality—and reflect on if there have been any shifts and synchronicities. Then take a deep dive into how you're feeling. Better? Same? Write it on the page.

Finally, think through your gratitude practice, and notice if there were any important moments or an "aha!" while you were doing it. Was there a specific practice that triggered something inside you? Did friends or family notice a difference in you while you were doing it? Write down any special events or insights that happened while you were Giving THANKS.

I noticed, as I did my own gratitude practice, that there were many big "aha" moments that I would have completely forgotten about had I not written them down. Writing about these special moments made me realize how much of an impact gratitude was making on me. What were the big moments for you while you were doing these practices? End your story by writing about those moments, both the small ones and the bigger ones, and how they led you to where you are right now.

This writing prompt is known as the "Then, Now, and How" format, and it's one of my favorites to use because it gives perspective on where you've been and how far you've come. And perspective is a powerful thing. When we have it, we can begin to see how everything in our lives is there to serve our highest and best purpose, always.

Once you're done writing your "Then, Now, and How" story on the journal pages provided, you can complete your gratitude journey by moving on to the last and final practice:

Writing your gratitude for the future.

MY GRATITUDE STORY

EPILOGUE:

THE FINAL GRATITUDE

There's one final, blank page here for you to write about something you're grateful for but that hasn't happened yet. Consider this to be the final chapter of your gratitude story, the part that's yet to be written. Your Epilogue.

ep·i·logue
noun

A short addition or concluding section at the end of a story, often dealing with the future of its characters.

This is an extremely powerful way to set your intention for what you'd like your future to look like. I use this practice myself every year around the New Year as a way to dream and set goals for the next year, five years, and beyond. Every year when I look back on my future gratitudes, I'm always amazed at how many have come to pass.

This practice is simple: Write about what you're grateful for that you want for the future. Think about the next month, year, or longer. Write as many things as you wish, and write them in the present tense, like they've already happened. For example, "I'm grateful for my amazing Hawaiian vacation with my family," if you've always wanted to travel there, or "I'm grateful that the world is at peace," if you want to extend your gratitude even further. Read them out loud to a trusted friend or loved one, or read them out loud to God.

Dream big.

Then tuck this journal away for a while, and come back to it to see how many future gratitudes have come true.

I promise, you'll be amazed at how many do.

GRATITUDE FOR THE FUTURE

"The simple act of practicing gratitude, consistently, is your invitation to a new life. Accepting the invitation is now up to you."

—FROM *THE GRATITUDE JAR: A SIMPLE GUIDE TO CREATING MIRACLES*